Meet Lady Liberty

Sharon Coan, M.S.Ed.

France is a country.

The United States is a country.

France gave the United States a gift.

The gift was a **statue**.

It is called the Statue of Liberty.

We call her Lady Liberty.

Liberty means **freedom.**

Lady Liberty came in many parts.

She is tall.

Her feet are big.

Her dress is long.

She holds a book.

She stands on an island.

The island is in New York.

She is **proud**.

She shows that we are free.

Make It!

1. Get some clay.
2. Make a statue about the United States.

3. Tell about it.

Glossary

freedom—the power to do what you want to do

proud—to feel happy about something you have done well

statue—art made out of clay, rock, or metal

Index

France, 2, 4

freedom, 8

New York, 15

statue, 5–6

United States, 3–4

Your Turn!

Lady Liberty shows that the United States is free. What else stands for freedom? Draw a picture.

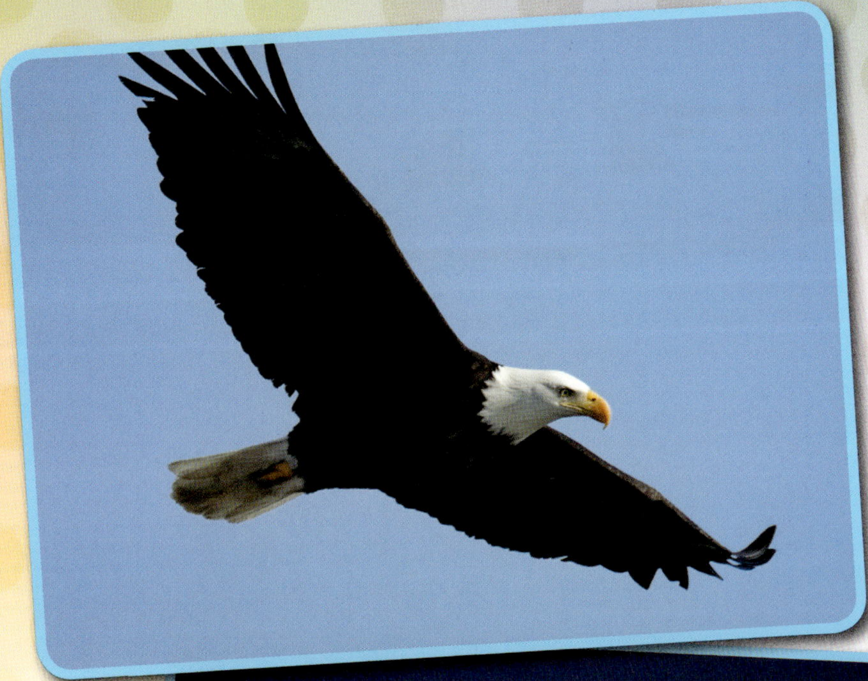

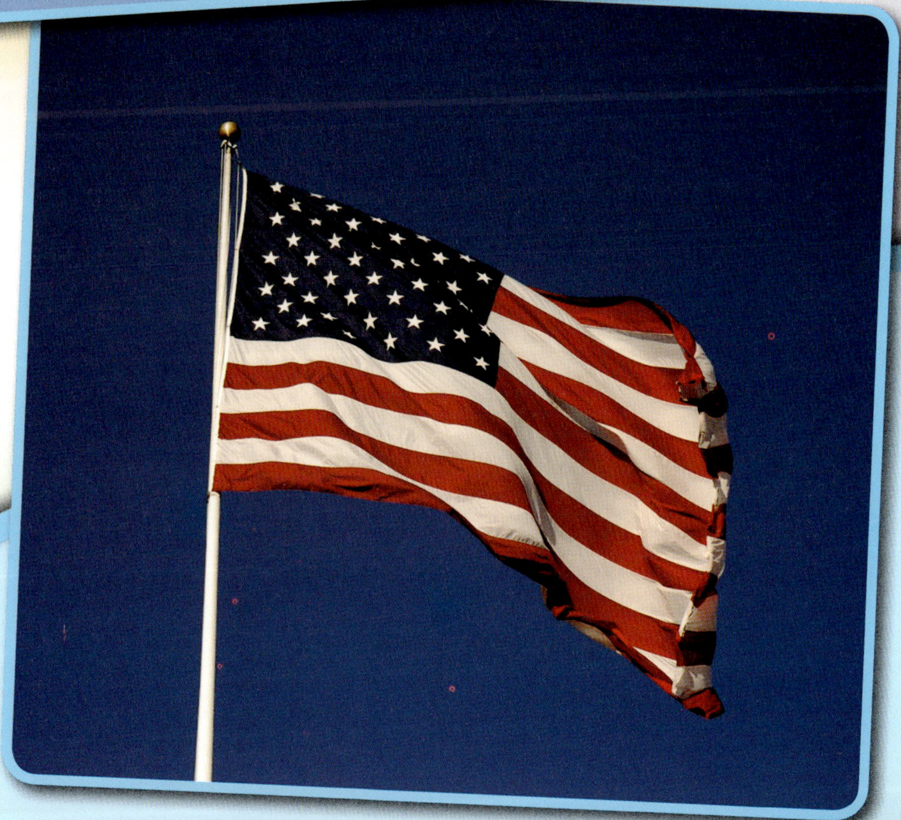

Consultants

Shelley Scudder
Gifted Teacher
Broward County Schools

Caryn Williams, M.S.Ed.
Madison County Schools
Huntsville, AL

Publishing Credits

Conni Medina, M.A.Ed., *Managing Editor*
Lee Aucoin, *Creative Director*
Torrey Maloof, *Editor*
Lexa Hoang, *Designer*
Stephanie Reid, *Photo Editor*
Rachelle Cracchiolo, M.S.Ed., *Publisher*

Image Credits: p.17 Travelwide/Alamy; p.19 Hillary Dunlap; p.22 Kena Betancur/Getty Images; p.10 Three Lions/Getty Images; pp.4, 9, 11 The Granger Collection, NYC; p.14 LOC [LC-DIG-highsm-16803]/The Library of Congress; p.5 LOC [LC-DIG-pga-04150]/The Library of Congress; All other images from Shutterstock.

Teacher Created Materials

5301 Oceanus Drive
Huntington Beach, CA 92649-1030
http://www.tcmpub.com

ISBN 978-1-4333-7340-4

© 2014 Teacher Created Materials, Inc.